Journey with Leonard
speaking child-like whispers, weaving wondering walks,
crafting new creation waters, carrying words penetrating deep
into memories awakening listeners to adventures revealing
Redeemer's finger prints covered over with wrinkles and
currents of time. Recall memories woven deep within and
dream again what the world will be like when we, stewards
of the earth, name so clearly the tears of humanity that all
hungry boys and girls receive daily bread and all God's children
joyfully join the birds of the air singing abundant songs of
thanksgiving and praise... for all fulfill Creator's purpose.

—*Rev. Dr. Bart W. Milleson, Senior Pastor*
Stallings United Methodist Church, Stallings, North Carolina

In his collection of poems, Leonard Fairley writes: "There is
so much more of earth's rare beauty to discover for those who
speak softly enough." The pulpit aside, Leonard is a quiet man
and it is that very quality that makes his book of poetry powerful, truthful, tender, inspiring, funny, human, surprising, and
sometimes difficult to hear. Read "Necessary Tools" first and let
go of words as you know them. Then listen for his own rare
beauty spoken softly into each and every line.

—*Susan N. Graebe, MDiv., Associate Director, ZOE Ministry*
(Zimbabwe Orphans Endeavor)

Gentle. Humble. Quiet. Loving. Leonard Fairley is all of these.
He is also a poet with a heart full of stories. *Who Shall Hear My
Voice?* is a powerful testimony to the strength of family, self-
determination, and God's blessings. Through a childhood filled
with challenges, to an adulthood as a trailblazer, Leonard has
lived many lives. "I ain't got the tools to tell you my dreams..."
begins one poem. I beg to differ. This collection of poems is
proof of Leonard's gift of language and story. May we all hear
his voice—rich in imagery, these poems proclaim LIFE!

—*Julie Brown, Print and Web Communications, Apex, North Carolina*

Who Shall Hear My Voice?

poems by

Leonard E. Fairley

Publications Unltd·

Raleigh, North Carolina

Who Shall Hear My Voice?
by Leonard E. Fairley
© Copyright 2009, Leonard E. Fairley

ISBN 13: 978-0-9767450-6-8
ISBN 10: 0-9767450-6-2
Library of Congress Control Number: 2009934426
First printing, 2009

To order, or for more information, please visit
http://www.poeticsay.com

Publishing Services by **Publications Unltd** · Raleigh, North Carolina
www.publicationsunltd.com

For my grandma Gladys,
my mother Doreatha,
and my wife Priscilla.
Wisdom, courage, and love
personified.

Blessings & Peace!

(signature)

Contents

Foreword   *vii*
Preface   *ix*

BEFORE ANY WORD IS SPOKEN
Today   3
The Office   4
The Zone   6
The Vision Tree   7
A Patch Of Blue   8
Keeping Faith   9
Whispered Conversations   10
The Miracle   11
A Chorus Of Water Falls   12
Before Any Word Is Spoken   13

NO WORDS FOR POWER
Necessary Tools   16
My Strong Desire   17
Such Are The Doubts Of Poets   18
Stuck   19
Why? Why Not?   20
Jesus With A Different Face   21
It Shall Be Revealed   22
Voices   24
Forgotten Words   26
When Will I Hear You Speak?   27
No Words For Power   29
Always Listening   30
Still There   31

CHILD'S HEART

Storm Is Passing Over   34

A Penny's Worth Of Trouble   36

The Bird's Nest   37

Under The Wild Cherry Tree   38

Easter Egg Hunt   39

"Not Even A Mouse"   40

Paper Sack Brown   41

JUSTICE DAY DREAMING

Phoenix Rising   44

Flower Unknown   45

No Room Left   46

Paradise   47

Different Eyes   49

Tear Drops   50

Christmas Eyes   51

Amber Broom   52

Marilyn Monroe 226 Center Street   53

My Father's Eyes   54

Fifty   56

Odessa   57

Foreword

PAY ATTENTION to the voices emanating from his soul, if you really want to know a man. And when he reveals his soul to you, be prepared for a surprisingly intimate awareness of the orb of life that surrounds him. A soul-man is aware of everything good and bad that shapes him. He can name these things. Leonard Fairley is a soul-man.

His poems tell you everything you need to know to convince you of this. When he tells you in "Amber Broom" about a grandmother weaving "troubles and hopes too fragile to be whispered into existence" into a house-sweeping broom, you may think they are not only hers, but his own. There is elation for the gift of an almond-eyed daughter in "Paper Sack Brown" whose presence gives him hope "when the colors of life seem to run together, and nothing is going right." And in "Marilyn Monroe 226 Center Street," he marvels at the hopeful vision of a "tiny black bombshell dressed for Easter, ghetto style," a poor black child whose dreams he suspects are as big as the name she bears.

Leonard Fairley's verse welcomes you into his inner journey to glimpse views of sadness tempered by hope, and disappointment countered by promise for a yet-to-be-fully-realized completeness of his life. Honest and masterfully insightful, the poems guide the reader into his or her own soulful look into the hollow places and the full places of ones life. Powerful enough that you will want to find a quiet place where you can read them again and again.

Dr. Steve Compton
Superintendent, Sanford District United Methodist Church
Author of Rekindling the Mainline *(The Alban Institute)*

Preface

I WAS AND IN MANY WAYS STILL REMAIN a classic day dreamer,
listening to the voices of life all around me. It was the only
way an introverted social outcast could make sense of the
world. Neither the first word nor the last word was mine to
speak. I daily struggled to come up with means by which to
draw attention away from myself, and yet within my soul a
voice screamed to be set free, to be heard. The first steps on the
journey were taken from "The Corner of The Invisible."
Society and the educational system fated me to such a place
where hopes were slowly swallowed up and voices silenced.
"The Corner of The Invisible" is that spot in every American
classroom where those least likely to succeed were out-of-sight,
and out-of-mind. It was from the corner of the invisible that I
first learned the magic of words. "See Spot run Jane, run Spot,
run," never did anything for me. However, fairy tales and Bible
stories (as unorthodox as it sounds) possessed the magic to
transport me from the worries of the day. In my silent corner
I could be anything, do anything, and go anywhere. The only
cost was to find the right words. I'd found my voice. The next
step on the journey was to develop the courage to share it.

Through the heartfelt, deeply personal words of this
volume of poetry God has graciously granted me the spiritual
inspiration needed in order to share the joys, the despair, the
celebrations and the struggles, the hopes and dreams of life.
Who Shall Hear My Voice? covers a wide range of experiences
that will hopefully remind the reader that all of creation has
a voice, and a longing to be heard. *Who Shall Hear My Voice?* is
a snapshot of my journey from voicelessness to liberation.

I give thanks to God that nothing can ultimately defeat
the power of a dream. My one dream amidst a life that
constantly spoke impossibilities was to find words to give
voice to experiences which daily cried out for expression.
Speaking one's existence is the magic of words dreamed
and spoken in silence. *Who Shall Hear My Voice?* contains
words that were once locked inside by fears, but are now

released in poetic hopes that they might unlock someone else's voice longing to be heard. Therefore, before any word is spoken, take delight in listening, and don't allow any power to strip away your dreams. Last, but not least, with a child's heart spend time working for simple justice.

I give God thanks for those people and experiences that became vital keys unlocking in me the courage to speak from the deep wells of my own longings. I especially give thanks to my wife Priscilla and my two children, Joshua and Elizabeth; from them I have truly learned that "The greatest of these is love." [I CORINTHIANS 13:13.]

—Leonard Fairley, August 2009

Before Any Word Is Spoken

Today

A moment of true joy,
strong enough to temper the
sorrows attempting
to dim its light.

A moment of deep laughter,
that shakes my soul
and washes me in tears
of delight.

A moment of recognized
grace, reminds me of
unconditional
love and care.

A moment of courage, to
live into all four and
the wisdom to understand.
These journeys we all share.

The Office

I've still as yet to learn your name,
But you're beautiful just the same.
Never have you held my ignorance
Against me, you've simple continued
To glow.

You catch my eye, daily stealing my
Breath away each time I walk into
This room filled with books and
Official documents, necessary items
For the way I make my living.

You hear my every whispered prayer,
Witness my anguished moods, the
Anxious laden tension filling every
Single muscle, mandated deadlines
Tighten their grip.

You know my heart's true desire is
To dance among your kind in native
Habitat, yet not a judgmental word
Falls from your tender leaves
Enticing me to follow my heart.

You sit with us at table conversations
Which turn to eager searching for
Elusive answers, yet you offer no
Spoken advice. You simply offer
Life flowing in deep roots.

I thought for certain I'd lost you lying
Overturned, prostrate upon the floor.
Leaves splayed wide around conference
Table legs, hours in silent agony.
Life drifting slowly away.

Inadequate shallow soil, hungry
Thirsty roots desiring nourishment.
Yet you never screamed, cursed, or
Shouted due to my neglect when I've
Lost myself in busyness.

I've still as yet to learn your name, but
You're beautiful just the same, especially
In your new home. Soil deep enough
For life giving roots. Resilient water
Flowing into every green leaf.

The Zone

"Let me make one thing perfectly clear."
The Nixon line is meant to grab your
Attention.

However, I do desire to make one thing
Clear, being in "the zone" is not limited to
Michael Jordan scoring fifty-five points.
Double Nickels against the New York
Knicks in Madison Square Garden among
Screaming basketball fanatics.

There are gardens of other kinds.
Gardens where both spirit and body
Find perfect peace, "the zone."

"Thin places" where time and space are
No longer barriers to true uninterrupted
Communion with the Divine.

A Southeastern North Carolina Long-
Leaf Pine forest on a slow not too humid
Summer day, now there's a zone.

A zone of a different kind, where summer's
Breeze blows through a million evergreen
Needles at once. The fingers of God strumming
An angelic harp.

A garden of a different kind that moves
You to a spiritual ecstasy that
No inflated ball going through a hoop
Can duplicate.

Would that I could, in this hectic world
Where the lines between sacred and profane
Have all but been erased, would that I could

Forever live in the zone, but alas no one
Not even MJ can be in the zone forever.
There is nothing wrong with hoping.

The Vision Tree

In the eyes of botany it was Quercus.
To the naked eye it was just an old tree,
a useless old Oak
standing against history's
powerful gust.

Botany said the life-blood of spring's sap
ceased rising in it veins long ago.
No new rings of age added to
the huge ancient trunk, secrets
kept in equally ancient sawdust.

Facts could not stop flowing tears
when metal teeth cut deeply
into the Vision Tree's heart.
Gnarled roots were perfect consolation,
comfort, and peace to eyes that could
care less about genus or age.

Roots of an old Oak tree
whispered in the soul.
"Stronger winds have I withstood."
Wisdom from a sage.

Metal grinding teeth of
progress cannot uproot stories
planted deeply, in soil
trodden upon by dreamers who
found a haven in the tangled, exposed
roots of Quercus—released from
Society's cage.

A Patch Of Blue

A patch of blue,
peeping through
heaven's gray
clouds, pregnant
spring's promised
showers.

A patch of blue,
eyes dancing,
waves ebbing,
mirroring black
pond water's
reflective power.

A patch of blue,
between green
water lilies, and
yellow blossoms,
bright colors
aquatic flowers.

A patch of blue,
clear enough to
make God blush
at creation's
own mirrored
reflection.

A patch of blue
from heaven's
black pond
water, God's
suspicious smile
of affection.

A patch of blue
on black
pond water,
cool morning
walks of contemplation.

Keeping Faith

Keeping faith with creation always gave me more
Than I deserved; rainbows in misty skies, wind
Blown songs from pine needle chimes, water
Cascading over changing stones, smells of
Rich field dirt newly sprinkled with rain.

Keeping faith with creation, life flowing hope
In the joy of a child's heart. I'd almost forgotten
The soothing peace found in mud oozing between
Naked toes after the roar of summer's violent storms.
"Peace in the valley" still reigns.

Keeping faith with creation always made my
Senses come alive with sights still able to send
My mind down paths of vivid daydreams, painting
Pictures of memories long thought dead, helping
Erase today's pain.

Keeping faith with creation is the air I breathe.
The hope that still causes shivers of promise like
Goose bumps to rise when I feel life has passed
Me by. It only takes the sound of a Mocking
Bird's roof top song to renew my faith, and
Keep me sane.

Whispered Conversations

Whispers at water's
edge, ripple of words
spoken, hopes by
someone discovered.
Whispered answers
against the wind,
secret treehouse
canopy. Lost among
hide-and-seekers,
hopes of being found.

Whispered questions
into ocean waves, crashing
against countless grains
of sand. Hoped for
answers on mountain peaks?
Water eroded beach
sand between naked toes,
tiny foot prints around
the magical sand castle
mound.

The Miracle

The flowering dogwood
Outside my office window.

The song of mockingbirds
Soaring from picket fence.

Fields of purple before
Being plowed earthen.

Universes undiscovered
Floating on dust balls.

Life in hopeless places
Hope against Hope.

A Chorus Of Water Falls

Harmonic voices escaping slate
Gray chapel walls, liberated songs
Flowing down mountain cliffs.
Journeys forming perfect praise
From nature's joyful tears.
Celebrations sung in the amazing
Key of a chorus of water falls.

Cascading droplets singing
Unique notes impossible to
Duplicate despite walls designed
For acoustical perfection.
Who can interpret such music?
Who can utter what they mean?
Angels are enthralled.

Rituals from Shaman lips, tomorrow's
Prophecy, sweet earthy melody from
Druid priestess. Rhetorical voices
Can never match flowing water's
Peaceful invitation to worship.
God's presence sings loud and clear
In a chorus of water falls.

Wash over me, baptize me, and set me
Free. Melt away my fear of silence
When words become useless.
I stand in awe at creations perfect song.
My soul Thirsts for encores of spiritual
Renewal, soulful contemplation from a
Chorus of water falls.

Before Any Word Is Spoken

Before any word is spoken,
may it be my joy to hear
the first bird song of
morning's dawn.

Before any word is spoken,
may it be my blessing to hear
the first breath of wind
blow through leaves still wet with
morning's dew.

Before any word is spoken,
may it be my joy to hear
each drop of spring's rain
touch the earth.

Before any word is spoken,
words that would profane
this sacred *thin place*,
may I be blessed.

May I be blessed before
the voice of the Creator becomes
lost in meaningless chatter.

No
Words
For Power

Necessary Tools

I ain't got the tools
to tell you my dreams.
Your dictionary ain't got
words to define what
my eyes done seen.

I ain't got the tools
to tell you my dreams.
I jus keep 'em to myself.
Your words too fancy
for the streets I walked, the
places I done been.

I ain't got the tools
to tell you my dreams.
Your words just ain't strong
enough to hold all the stuff
that needs to be screamed.

I ain't got the tools
to tell you my dreams.
Your words like quicksand
swallow them up
jus as fast as I can dream 'em.

My Strong Desire

Is it possible to desire to
see so clearly until
you're blind?

I desire your presence so
strongly Lord, until I've
missed you in a thousand places.

Is it possible to desire to
hear a voice so clearly until
you're deaf?

I desire to hear your voice
Lord Jesus, until I've
failed to hear it in a thousand sounds.

Am I afraid of how you might look?
Am I afraid of what you might say?
Forgive me Lord!

Open my eyes that I might see.
Open my ears that I might hear.
This is my one desire.

Such Are The Doubts Of Poets

When words lose their beauty,
Texting is much more convenient.
Who cares if letters are missing?
Nothing is lost.

When words are taken out of context.
Sound bites equal ratings, equal money.
Twenty-four-seven news needs to be
Fed at all cost.

When words lose their integrity.
Semantics always trumps truth.
Heart and soul no longer speak.
Who will pay the price prophetic
Words exact?
    The Poet
     Suffers
      Most!

Stuck

They are stuck there.

Scars of past pain
pick their time to
re-emerge when trust
is a possibility.

Stuck there
as memories of
shot-gun houses;
sheltered in captivity.

Flashbacks of malnourished
outstretched hands begging
for a stick of butter to flavor
a pot of rice.

Stuck there
without expression,
crying out to be heard.
I've screamed into
darkness, hungry attempts
at revealing poverty's
ugly vice.

They are stuck there.
Longing for new strength
a voice better, able,
loud enough, to be
heard.

Why? Why Not?

God don't let me forget this dream!
Not a dream of images, a dream
of two simple questions:
Why? Why Not?

Is the child in me now dormant?
Have I forgotten or am I just afraid?
It is not the grown-up thing to do.

Why not ask why?
When the tears of pain sting your cheeks.
Why not ask why?
Words cannot explain.

God don't let me forget this dream!
Not a dream of fame and fortune,
a dream of two simple questions.
Why? Why Not?
Why not dream "the impossible?"

Have I come to believe the myth?
"Dreams are for those who sleep?"
If not the dreamer, who will find the
courage to ask why, prophetically
crying why not?

God don't let me forget this dream!
Not a dream born from a place
of power, a dream of two simple questions:
Why? Why not?

Why not dream of things not as they are
but of how they can, and should, be?
We've silenced the why of the poor.
Silenced the why and why not of the dreamers,
silenced them as childhood foolishness.

Why make impossible the hopes and dreams of why not?
Not a dream of business as usual.
A dream bold enough to speak into the
face of convention and reality.

Why?
Why not?

Jesus With A Different Face

I keep looking down the dirt road trying to see
If Jesus is coming. Just a glimpse of his glorious
Silhouette against the evening's afterglow would
Be satisfactory.

Will the haze of mankind's weapons of mass
Destruction obstruct my view? The ozone layer
Certainly wouldn't be an obstacle. Its protection
Is no longer a factor.

"Behold I stand at the door and knock." My
Ear has been pressed against the door so long.
I am afraid it might be too numbed. Jesus will
Have to speak louder.

I thought about switching ears. However, my
Good ear is filled with too many other sounds;
Curses, deceit, lies and arrogant chatter drowning
Out Jesus.

I am afraid we would never recognize a voice
Calling for peace, truth, and justice. Lord knows,
Forget about love. The meaning of the word has
Been completely spoken out of it.

Nothing like this blocked my eyes or interfered
With my ears in younger yesteryears. There in
Evening's afterglow walked Jesus, strides wide
Enough to cross any divide.

I looked down the dirt road, and there walked
Jesus brown skin, slender legs, two brown paper
Sacks underneath weary arms. Between the furrows
Of that brow lies a deep hope strong enough to fill
Any need.

What I hear despite the gulf of distance between us
Is the hum of a familiar song; "Precious Lord Take
My Hand." Today Jesus has my mama's voice:
The
    Promise
         Of
            My
               Only
                  Meal!

It Shall Be Revealed

Speak softly upon the earth.
Imagine what healing music
We've missed drowned in
Noises—self-conceived.
Longings for leisure, recreation
And luxury created to ease
Troubled hearts.

How many hearts must suffer
Constant, daily pounding?
Consumer driven busy work,
Producing massive anxiety
Laden heart attack.
What healing has lost its
Power in the shouting?

There is so much more of
Earth's rare beauty to
Discovery for those who
Dare speak softly enough.
Listen to what is revealed.
True peace is found only
In such moments.

Live simply upon the earth.
She will reveal scarcity
Is a myth, manufactured
Justification for hoarding
Earth's blessings.
Treasures shared by all.
We must live simply
So that others can simply live.

Truer words have never been
Spoken. The *Word* must become
Flesh living among us. Feed the
Hungry, clothe the naked. *Give*
Us our daily bread. The *Word*
Sounds so foreign when individualistic
Greed is the American creed.

Live peaceable upon the earth.
She will reveal ownership
Is an illusion igniting short
Fuses. Future warheads
Recklessly rising from silos
Concealed in hearts of covetous
Minds drunk on strange wine.

Selfish fruit, speaking absolute
Truths erecting senseless barriers.
If my way is wrong nobody
Is right. If I cannot own
The world nobody will.
My birthright makes it just
Fine.

Voices

Where have all the prophets gone?
"The voices of those crying in the
Wilderness." Trapped behind stain glass
Windows covered on altars beneath
Beautiful paraments, hearts concealed
Behind Preacher's robes and stoles
Too thick.

"The Word made flesh," open
Pulpit Bibles all to see the words
Of Jesus printed in red, scattered
By ill winds from pages often
Left to mold in empty sanctuaries,
Mildew strong enough to make
You sick.

The Word walks by everyday
Pushing a cart collecting trash,
Trying to live from day-to-day
Hoping someone will hear—someone
Will see. The Wildman drifting
From place to place, bottle to needle,
Smoke to pill with no one to care.

The Word walks by everyday.
The girl who needs no scarlet
Letter, her fall clear enough
For all to see, etched across
Her face in premature wrinkles;
Far away eyes, beauty crying
Desperately for love to share.

Where have all the prophets gone?
Clouds of doubts shadow assurance.
I doubt I'd recognize such a one unless
They spoke in familiar terms of effective
Leadership, and prosperity, exclusive
Social clubs. Where are your credentials?
Where is your get out of hell card?

The flock has no choice but drink from
Hell's stagnant fountain, blind prophets
Lead them there on false future promises.
Prophets wearing politicians clothing
Usurping holy voice. The church has
Sold her birthright when responsibilities
Become too hard.

Where have all the prophets gone?
Buried beneath polished armor of
Individual piety and righteous
Prayers to save their souls—forget the
World. When will prophets speak
Truth again as heaven's hopeful
Ward?

Forgotten Words

Making a living, instead of living.
I've learned the lesson all too well.
How much longer can my spirit
Endure this lie I've forced upon myself?

My entire body groans beneath the
Weight of words I no longer recognize.
Where are yesterday's words that spoke
So clearly?

I thought I'd locked them deep inside.
Protection strong enough preserving
Sanity. Future hopes of possibilities
Long since forgotten.

Dreams are what I presently call them.
Before today they were more than real not
Shadows of their former selves. Words
Powerful enough, sending my soul dancing

With anticipation. Such words no longer
Apply. I've sinfully replaced them with
Vocabulary lacking imagination, words
Capable of putting food on the table.

Words begin as necessity have grown into
Wordless cancer spreading like wild fire,
Destroying what was meant to be. I hardly
Recognize what remains.

A shell of my past, present, future self.
I've journeyed from destiny's path traveling
On dreamless roads, searching for signpost
Pointing forward. *The Word Made Flesh.*

When Will I Hear You Speak?

I long to hear your voice,
not in some mysterious kind of way,
but in a voice that a hungry
child can understand.

In the silence I found
courage to carve out a
small piece of hope
or was that your voice?

*Is it a blasphemous desire to want
to hear the voice of God?*

I long to hear your voice,
not in some hocus-pocus kind of way,
but in a voice that a child
orphaned by war can understand.

The screaming voices of millions, possibly
billions shout into the darkness.
Is this your voice?
If war is your voice, I will stop my ears
no matter how loud the war drums beat.

I long to hear your voice,
not in some magical kind of way,
but in a voice a child marked for
genocide can understand.

The screaming voices of millions, possibly
billions shout into the darkness.
Are the circumstances of my
birth, race, gender, ethnicity
enough to
render me voiceless?
Why can't I live and not die?

*Is it a blasphemous desire to want
to hear the voice of God?*

—continued

I long to hear your voice,
not in some mysterious, hocus-pocus,
magical kind of way, but in
the voice of a child longing
for assurance of real hope.

Millions, possibly billions
scream in the darkness,
listening for a word from you.

Is it a blasphemous desire to want
to hear the voice of God?

I long to hear your voice,
not in some mysterious, hocus-pocus,
magical kind of way
but in a voice a child crying
in the darkness can understand.

No Words For Power

I have no words to speak to power.
My words were always those of poverty.
My heart is that of the poor.
I fear power will never understand.

I have no mind for power.
My mind was occupied by poverty.
My heart is that of the poor.
I fear power never thinks the irrational thoughts
of life from hand-to-mouth.

I have no eyes for power.
For too long, my eyes have wept for the poor.
My heart is that of poverty.
I fear power shall forever be blind, rendering
invisible the poor,
waving,
    shouting,
        begging
to be seen.

I have no heart for power.
My heart is scarred too deeply.
My heart is that of the poor.
I fear that power is too heartless
to loosen its grip.

Always Listening

The call of blue jays echoing down
tree-lined sidewalk streets. If only I
could get a glimpse of one
I could rest my craning neck.

The rhythm of wind blowing in
tree top branches. I listen with
all my soul for music's
heavenward trek.

The echo of dogs barking on crisp nights,
Winter's cold breathe amplified territorial
communications, penetrating the walls
of my darkened room.

I try to decode the sounds.
Hope might ride in on the whispers of a blue jay.
Hope may ride in on the still small voice,
Not some thunderous boom.

I dare not miss the possibility of
some inaudible whispered words
helping hopes, and dreams come true
riding upon the wind.

Hope may sound in the distant
chirp of crickets' legs
racing a million times
per second blowing my mind.

Still There

I think they are still there,
dreams of my childhood.
Weak echoes I thought
long buried.
Voices slowly, courageously
rising to be
set free.

I want so badly to be set free.
Is that possible, after
buying into the world's
reality?

I hope they are still there.
Maybe I lost the keys or
never possessed them.
Or was it a dream?

I cry out to you Creator,
whoever
you
are.

Let it not be a
CRY
INTO
DARKNESS!

A
Child's
Heart

Storm Is Passing Over

Boy, come down out of that tree,
ain't you got no sense to see a
cloud is coming up? Show respect!
The Lord is fixin' to work.

Unplug that T.V., cut off
all those lights.
Can't you hear the thunder roll?
Ain't you got no ears to hear?
The Lord is fixin' to work.

Sit down somewhere, hush
your mouth and be still.
Ain't you got no respect,
don't you fear the Lord?
The Lord is fixin' to work.

Hush, don't even think about
opening your mouth or moving
a muscle till this cloud
done passed over this house.
The Lord is fixin' to work.

Don't you test me or the Lord!
Just because it's dark in here, this
switch can still sting
so you better hush and
don't start that playing.
The Lord is fixin' to work.

When the non-believer dared to
speak, lighting struck from the
end of her switch with the flick
of her ancient wrist. Moses is
an old black woman.

Hush, I said, when the Lord is
working, y'all got plenty time to run
your mouth and play when this
storm is done passed over.
The Lord is working now.

Silent hush falls over the
unbelievers huddled in the
darkened room, whispered
prayers from sacrilegious
hearts, "Lord finish your work."

No wimpy: "rain, rain go away."
Hush Lord, and finish your work
ain't you got no heart for children
who want to play?

Hush Lord, and pass over; finish
your work, there are mud puddles
and swollen creeks waiting for
toes and feet to romp and stomp.
Please, let the storm pass over.

A Penny's Worth Of Trouble

I dropped a penny
in an empty lamp receptor.
I witnessed stars in the
Milky Way, exploding
chaotic streams of
colored sparks.

I dropped a penny
in an empty lamp receptor.
I witnessed what God must
have seen before the word
spoke light. The empty void
called dark.

I dropped a penny
in an empty lamp receptor.
I heard what Adam and Eve
heard, a voice calling, echoing
through the run-down shack.
"Where art thou hiding?"

I dropped a penny
in an empty lamp receptor.
I felt like screaming into the
midst of this rising storm.
"Noah, save me from this
storm, on a boat ride."

I dropped a penny
in an empty lamp receptor.
Nothing, not even Noah
could save me from the
stripes I would surely
receive to my narrow hide.

I dropped a penny
in an empty lamb receptor,
still plugged into the electric
wall socket, carrying at least 220.
A house once alive with living
light immediately just died.

The Bird's Nest

Dog days of summer,
mercury going hay wire,
lucky me. My feet have
memories of yesterday's
Summer treat.

Dog days of summer,
sun baked grains of sand
hill dirt to make your
feet sizzle feeling like
grilled meat.

Dog days of summer,
who thought of such
a name? The bird's
nest a haven where
skinny dippers meet.

The bird's nest,
what genius named
it a night club? Dancing
weekend clubber's
pulsing night beats?

The bird's nest,
forbidden to sun burned
feet daring not to tread
past the threshold no matter
how bold the feat.

The bird's nest,
black shimmering refreshing
pond water, sediment of
fallen leaves too deep for
the faint or weak.

The bird's nest,
lean dark bodies swimming
shore to shore toward
high mud banks. Graceful
strokes never missing a beat.

Under The Wild Cherry Tree

The garbage dumpster behind Firestone
Always had a few refrigerator boxes big
Enough for two small boys on hands and
Knees, down hill tanks rolling over blades
Of green snow. The perfect toy.

Mr. "Bub" Stewart's Gulf service
Station always had a few worn out car
Tires, perfect down hill racing size,
Guided at top speed by tiny fingers unafraid
Of possible injury enraptured by perfect joy.

The corner of Gulf and Pine always had
A single solitary street light beneath
Soft luminous rays where voices echoed
Against the surrounding summer night.
What will be tomorrow's plight?

Whatever futures dawn might bring they
Will forever be sweeter even as memories
Beneath bitter sweet succulent fruit.
The sound of rolling cardboard tanks over
Green grass. The rumble of tires on asphalt
Streets. Under the Wild Cherry Tree all is
Right.

Easter Egg Hunt

Wading ankle deep among
Tender new spring grass.
Seeking brightly colored
Objects of every child's
Affection.

Eyes scanning wide with
Anticipatory delight.
Peripheral vision working
Over-time, capturing every
Minute reflection.

Radiant golden plastic
Egg filled with candy.
Grand prize strategically,
Gracefully cradled among
Dogwood blossoms.

Pleading fingers reaching,
Toward the sacred sight.
Careful not to draw attention.
Standing on naked tip toes
Inches away from awesome.

"Not Even A Mouse"

The perfect tree makes all the difference no matter
That it comes from the wrong of side of the CSX
Railroad tracks. Huge Christmas bulbs draped
Across its branches dancing in brown eyes should
Have been the give-a-way.

The perfect Christmas despite the usual sleeping
Arrangements; four at the foot, three at the head,
The youngest two on a pallet at the foot of my
Mama's bed.

Heat from a pot belly stove stirred the smell of
Christmas apples, oranges, and candy. Sweet
Aromas floating from a secure place safe from
Tiny fingers that cannot possible survive the
Temptation, forbidden fruit still has that power.

We had no earthly idea what sugar plums were.
What danced in our heads was the joy of new
Toys, not those from "the toy train" of
Christmases past.

Toys from generous hearts or crying eyes,
Children who didn't want to give up their old
Toys, despite their need for repair before poor
Hands would love them back to life on Christmas
Day.

It wasn't the "coo of little Cindy Lou Who,"
But pent-up excitement or was it truly fear.
"There is a rat in the apples," not even a
Mouse.

In a flash we were up, the rat forgotten all
Eyes now on the first new store-bought toys
We'd ever received. Yes, Sheila and Vanessa
There is Santa Claus!

Paper Sack Brown

Color my heart paper sack brown.
The miracle arrived with almond
shaped eyes, and tiny slender
fingers ready for a million
telephone conversations.

Color my heart paper sack brown.
Head full of hair moving in every direction,
caught up in heavenly breezes that
blew in with her on this journey,
making my life complete.

Color my heart paper sack brown,
only that shade makes it all
worth while when the colors of
life seems to run together, and
nothing is going right.

Color my heart paper sack brown.
I am blessed knowing that
Elizabeth Nicole is in the world.

Justice
Day Dreaming

Phoenix Rising

Fireplace ashes, morning's
Warmth. Seven children,
Two adults seeking
comfort from winter's
icy touch
longing for May.

Sweet potatoes buried
Beneath waning noon gray
Embers, hoped for nourishment
Sustaining empty groaning
Stomachs one more day.

Yesterday's ashes cold dead
Dirt to more fortunate eyes.
Care worn hands submerged
In lye soap water, cleaning
Hand-me-downs covering
Nearly naked bodies best
They can.

Evening's red embers baking
Dutch oven "hoecakes" kneaded
Flour, grease, and water, survival
Magic from thin female fingers
Making a way despite a no good
Piece of man.

Smothering fireplace ashes,
Healing incubator warmth,
Soothing the whispering cries
Of a premature baby, scorching
The weary legs of a tireless
Seemingly invincible woman.

Phoenix rising from
fireplace ashes.
No myth!
No metaphor!
Life!

Flower Unknown

Unfolding each spring in poverty's fields of
Dreams, flowers unknown.
Mystic beauty in ghetto streets amidst
Empty wine bottles and used syringes,
Blooms the promise of flowers unknown.

In festering crevices of ghetto garbage,
Soiled pampers, liquid crack "forties" and
Used condoms, dreams miraculously
Reaching skyward in soil of crime and grime.
Blooms the promise of flowers unknown.

Had they always been so beautiful?
Small malnourished hands pulling them
Against sunken brown cheeks, leaving
Yellow star marks wherever its golden
Petals touch, a flower unknown.

Barefoot children running in hopes
Of desolate fields bringing joy to
Streets paved with injustices no child
Should endure. What dreams bloom
In the promise of flowers unknown?

What happened to all those flowers
Playing kickball in the midst of this
Ghetto, screaming with unbridled laughter,
Sensing beauty seldom noticed in richer
Fields? Flowers unknown.

I wonder if they are growing in
Brighter fields, reaching skyward
In the midst of impossible odds?
Yellow stars imprinted on plump
Cheeks, promise in full bloom.

No Room Left

The world has no room
For any more sorrow. The
Floods wait for no tomorrow.
They will simply have to flow
Inward. There is no more space
To borrow.

The world has no room for
Senseless shedding of blood,
Its spilling is an evil flood.
The rhetoric of voices alone
Are powerless to stop blood's flow
As Long as greed is the creed.

The world has no room for
All the pain. The hurt will
Simply sink deeper into burden
Hearts, its sorrowful weight
Added to an already enormous
Gain.

The world has no room for
Midnight eyes that weep
A million tears. Soul water,
Deep enough for renewal
Losing its cleansing power to
Transform the darkness of fear.

When will sorrows cease to flow?
When will pain cease to grow?
When will blood no longer smear?
Can perfect love cast out fear?
Can the world these hopes sustain?

Paradise

What all-wise God would create
paradise placing within it's very
heart creatures with passions,
hopes, dreams, needs, and wants
powerful enough to call forth death's
darkness?

What all-knowing God would
expect creatures with the motto,
"I think therefore, I am" to find
rest on the Sabbath when doing is
better than being? "I am therefore,
I do."

God might be able to get away
with working just six days.
I am human, my work
is never done. There aren't
ever enough hours in a day
to get it all done.
What creative God would
give dominion of a perfectly
good world to a creature newly
born? "The garden is yours, you
only get one lifetime to make
it work."

"Try not to mess it up!"
"No you cannot eat from
the tree of good and evil,
definitely not from the
tree of life; remember,
one lifetime only."

What jealous God would
create a human so easily
distracted by counterfeit
beauty, devoting its soul
to all that glitters as though
it was gold, or possibly God?

—continued

This planet is full of gods,
worshipped as worthy enough
for killing, genocide,
oppression, ethnic cleansing,
gods absolute, and unwilling
to share paradise.

What image-casting God would
reveal us as being created in
God's image? War, fear,
hatred and violence can blind
so completely. We neither
see nor hear the mirror image
    Screaming while
        Life's blood
        Flees
        Paradise!

Different Eyes

When once I saw with different eyes,
possibilities flowed instead of tears.

When once I saw with different eyes,
days to come had no room for fears.

When once I saw with different eyes,
strife and war were no where near.

When once I saw with different eyes,
hope, joy, and love were always clear.

Eyes not blinded by me-ism.
Eyes not inhibited by the bottom line.

Eyes not clouded by prejudice.
Eyes not afraid to see the light.

When once I saw with different eyes,
I was never afraid to dance in the light.

Tear Drops

Behold the universe in tear drops.
Africa's weeping children, AIDS
Flowing in dual droplets descending
down black cheeks stained with
hopeless water, when they should be kissed.

Behold the universe in tear drops.
Katrina's wrath in a wheel chair,
too many tears for government
Kleenex to wipe away a daughter's
loss. Who will weep for the missed?

Behold the universe in tear drops.
Iraq's children, tears falling on weapons
of mass destruction; too many tears
mixed in desert sands while
war's evil is hissed.

Behold the universe in tear drops.
A weeping world dropping soundless
moisture in thirsty pools of hope too
deep for talking heads to analyze, radical
agape blows a hopeful kiss.

Christmas Eyes

In the eyes of a Bethlehem Jewish Baby,
God gazes upon the world for the very first
Time through human eyes.

In the scream of a new born baby delivered
In the cave of shepherds' field, God speaks
For the very first time with human voice.

In the powerful tender grip of a baby's fingers
Intertwined with those of homeless parents,
God holds fast to creation.

Who could have believed the cost of such
A grip would be nail prints, bloodstained
Tears, cries of abandonment?

    What
        Child
            Indeed
                    Is
                        This!

Amber Broom

Straw brush broom, sun light faded semblance
Of yesterday's amber color. Straw brush broom,
Standing in plank board rooms collecting unseen
Dust mites, insects and dreams. Unafraid spiders
Weaving geometric webs no need rushing to
Complete.

Straw brush broom, powerful enough to sweep
Yards free of unwanted debris. Naked, bare not
A blade of grass, silent without purpose.
What hands would dare pick it up today
When electric or gas powered leaf blowers can
Do the job making Ben-Gay obsolete?

Grandma's hands skilled at crafting practical
Gadgets, beautiful in their own right. Grandma's
Wicker chair, favored spot for such spiritual work,
Strong enough to bare all her cares and concerns.
Contemplation's quiet song is woven from places
Heaven alone knows absolute.

Desires, dreams, despair and suffering, sweet
Soulful hums containing groans deep enough,
Speaking what can only be spoken through
Weary fingers weaving amber brooms. She weaves
Troubles and hopes too fragile to be whispered
Into existence. This amber broom sweeps away pain.

Enough healing remains in that old broom
For those who'd dare pick it up for sweeping,
Humming some unknown song releasing some
Hurt, conceiving some dream. What long ago
Dreams of mine remain while sweeping
Grandma's yard?

Marilyn Monroe 226 Center Street

Marilyn Monroe, 226 Center Street,
Tiny black bombshell dressed for Easter,
Ghetto style. How did she come to this?
Glamour doesn't belong on this street.

Marilyn Monroe in ebony.
How did she come to this?
Obsidian jewel parading down
asphalt runways on slender feet.

Marilyn Monroe in miniature.
How did she come to this?
What gift did they find in that name?
Will it erase the shame?

Marilyn Monroe with kinky hair.
How did she come to this?
Royal Crown such hair can tame.
Is it all just some game?

Marilyn Monroe, 226 Center Street.
Maybe the name is a gift that will
help this child rise above the shame.
In her eyes I see the dream that needs no
glamorous name.

Marilyn Monroe is a poor black child
with dreams just as big. I am in love
just the same.

My Father's Eyes

It has never been said that
I have my mother's eyes,
could it possibly be that
I see with my father's eyes?

My father's eyes, did they
ever look out school room
windows caught wide-eyed
in a day dream?

Did they ever follow
the delicate dance of
a free wind borne
butterfly?

Did they ever witness
The hypnotic spell of
an ocean wave crashing
ashore?

It has been said that my father's
eyes were clouded by pain, suffering,
and hopelessness caused by ebony
skin.

My father's eyes, were they
forever blinded by alcohol's
toxic poison trying to kill the
pain?

What did they see when
they were sober? Eyes
of promise, hope's bright
future.

I will always believe
they once danced,
delighted and filled
with life's passion.

My father's eyes have
long since ceased to
dance, life's rhythm
silenced.

Sight cut short, yet so
so much more of
life to see, gone too
soon.

My father's eyes, I'd
give anything that he
might see through my
eyes.

I'll drink in every ounce
Of life's water, living
it to absolute fullness,
with eyes wide open.

It has never been said that
I have my mother's eyes,
could it possibly be that
I see with my father's eyes?

Fifty

I've witnessed it a thousand times.
The flap of its powerful wings positioning it
soaring. I stare in awe witnessing
the first time a Hawk.

I've witnessed these mountains
this valley countless times. Where heaven
meets earth at mountain peak. I stare
amazed the first time, I gawk.

I've witnessed it a million times,
ocean and horizon meet in seamless
flow. I stare through a child's eyes. The first
time majesty's might.

I've seen a million human faces,
"red and yellow, black and white."
Universal star dust musical harmony,
dancing in creation's light.

I've journey many miles.
I've spent too much of life
Judging, analyzing, and rationalizing.
What have I missed due to fear?

Let go, take the plunge.
Fifty is the perfect time to
live passionately. Living out
wisdom's years.

March 29, 1957 – March 29, 2007:
What a great day to empty yourself,
planting your weary feet firmly on
rainbow arches without shedding a tear.

Live life as if for the first time
No worries about journey's end.
Don't blow fifty more with destiny
near.

Odessa

If rhythm is a dancer her name is Odessa.
Phonograph needle gliding across soulful
Ebony forty-fives that's all it took to behold the
Creative power in slender hips.

Dancing goddess' pearly whites popping
Wrigley Spearmint in rhythm with
Motown hits. It's an intoxicating spell
including ruby lips.

Pulsating rhythms capturing
both spectator and dancer.
Joyfully I surrender soul and heart.
Odessa takes me on an amazing trip.

"Soul Music" is the only word
powerful enough to describe sweet release
flowing in grandma's front room.
Spinning black gold the goddess holds.

No drug could contain the dance of
Odessa's soul. Better to sin in the sanctuary,
grandma holy of holies, than in some
den of iniquity.

What Goddess needed drugs?
Her body was the magic dream weaver
calling forth captivating movements.
Perfect unmatched equity.

If rhythm is a dancer, freedom is its
name, nothing on earth or in heaven
hindered such unbridled pent-up joy.
The snap of narrow fingers tips.

I can visualize the creator's joy
at the amazing wonder of this creature's
worshipful ability to cast such a gripping
spell with just the sway of her hips.